Lay Leaders Manual

Conference and District

Lay Leaders Manual

DISCIPLESHIP RESOURCES
PO BOX 340003 • NASHVILLE, TN 37203-0003
www.discipleshipresources.org

ISBN
Print 978-0-88177-698-0
Mobi 978-0-88177-699-7
Epub 978-0-88177-700-0

Library of Congress Control Number: 2013958432

Printed in the United States of America

DR 698

CONTENTS

A Call to Ministry

"All Christians are called through their baptism to this ministry of servanthood in the world to the glory of God and for human fulfillment" (*BOD*). By virtue of our baptism we are called into mission and ministry in the world and in the church. It is mission and ministry and not a "job" or position. "Every layperson is called to carry out the Great Commission (Matt. 28:18-20); every layperson is called to be missional" (*BOD*).

It is important that both the clergy and the laity realize this fact and that we live out our ministry as we have been gifted and called whether it is in the factory or the hospital; at work or at home; in the church or in the community. We are all God's people in all places, and in all times, and we are called to love and to serve.

Scriptural Basis

The scriptural basis that supports our call is found in 1 Peter 2:9, the Priesthood of Believers: "But you are the ones chosen by God, chosen for the high calling of priestly work, chosen to be a holy people, God's instruments to do his work and speak out for him, to tell others of the night-and-day difference he made for you—from nothing to something, from rejected to accepted" (1 Peter 2:9, The Message). The author was not just speaking to priests but to all followers of the way. The passages about spiritual gifts and the body of Christ in 1 Corinthians 12 suggest that all who desire to follow Christ and are baptized receive the spiritual gifts from God in order to accomplish the work of mission and ministry in the world

Purpose

What is the purpose of our call to mission or ministry? It is to provide workers for the harvest (Luke 10:2 and Matt. 9:37) and to go into the world making disciples and baptizing them in the name of Jesus (Matt. 28:18-20). While we are not all called to be evangelists and missionaries as our full-time vocations, we are all called to be disciples and to help form others as disciples. We are all called to demonstrate God's love to a hurting and lost world.

History

As United Methodists we have a rich heritage of the important role of the laity in mission and ministry. Class leaders and class meetings were the hallmark of early Methodism. They were an effective means of providing nurture to and oversight of the members of the Methodist societies. Class leaders were assigned to watch over the members in their class meetings with love. They were to visit each person in the class once a week to inquire how their souls "prospered" and provide any encouragement or instruction that the person needed. Class leaders then met with the minister once a week to inform him of those who were sick or in need of spiritual guidance.

Lay exhorters also participated in leadership roles during the society meetings. They led prayers, spoke on the subject of religion, encouraged and admonished other members of the group, described their own experience, and testified to their present joy. Lay exhorters did not preach regularly, but they were called upon to preach when the pastor or circuit rider (in early American Methodism) failed to show up.

Appointed a band leader at the Foundry, Thomas Maxfield went from exhorter to lay preacher. He began preaching—or "taking a text"—in the absence of John Wesley. When Wesley learned that Maxfield was unhappy, Wesley spoke with his mother who said, "Take care what you do with respect to that young man; for he is as surely called of God to preach as you are. Examine what have been the points of his preaching and hear him yourself." Upon hearing Maxfield preach Wesley exclaimed, "It is the Lord! [L]et him do what seemeth him good. What am I that I should withstand God?"

In early Methodism the laity were involved in other areas of leadership. While women did not usually hold leadership or pastoral roles, Susannah Wesley held Bible studies and training sessions in the rectory of Epworth and alarmed her husband, Samuel, by the "irregularity" of her fireside services.

Sarah Crosby, appointed a class leader, became one of the first female preachers in Methodism. The idea of women in leadership and preaching roles was highly controversial in the eighteenth century. It was a major step for John Wesley to acknowledge the validity of a woman's call to preach. He did encourage Crosby to speak publicly about her faith but cautioned her against speaking from a biblical text. "Never speak in a continued discourse–intermix short exhortations with prayer. Keep as far from what is called preaching as you can," Wesley advised. Wesley also gave Mary Bosanquet permission to preach on account of her "extraordinary call."

John Wesley became so convinced of the ability of the laity to preach and teach that he finally said, "Give me one hundred preachers who fear nothing but God, and I care not a straw whether they be clergymen or laymen, such alone will shake the gates of hell and set up the kingdom of heaven on earth."

Class/Society Members

Every member of a Methodist society or class was to be involved in mission and ministry. They were to visit the sick and imprisoned, feed the hungry, care for strangers, and do all the good they could do in the world. United Methodists today carry on the tradition of laity called to mission and ministry.

United Methodists are:

A covenant people who vow to uphold the church with their prayers, their presence, their gifts, their service, and their witness;

Diverse, committed to inclusiveness, and celebrating of different people, cultures, and histories;

Biblical in their faith and guided by scripture, tradition, experience, and reason;

Mission-oriented, aware of world events, and committed to helping those in need;

Socially conscious and people who work for world peace and justice;

Ecumenical and people who work with other denominations to spread the gospel, care for those in need, alleviate injustice, and foster peace;

Personally involved and people who strive to help the worker, the sick, the poor, the orphaned, the aging, the oppressed, and the imprisoned as they have since the days of John Wesley;

Connectional (The United Methodist Church is organized to carry out the mission of the church at the local, district, conference, jurisdictional, national, and global levels);

Evangelical and committed to the "spread of scriptural holiness";

Accountable disciples committed to practicing the Means of Grace and witnessing to the love of Christ though acts of compassion, justice, worship, and devotion;

Lay Servants who lead the church through the ministries of leading, caring, and communicating.

Reflection Questions

Think about your call to ministry and mission. In what ways do you, as a layperson, continue to listen or look for ways that God is leading you to fulfill this call?

Leadership Development

Spiritual leadership is a critical component of leadership within the church. All leaders should be aware of their visibility and the opportunity they have to model discipleship. Leaders must be intentional in their own spiritual development before they can lead others.

Tools for Spiritual Leadership

Our Wesleyan heritage gives us an excellent method for caring holistically for our spiritual growth.

John Wesley admonishes us in the General Rules to do no harm, do good, and to attend upon the ordinances of God which he called the Means of Grace—the spiritual disciplines through which we maintain our relationship with Christ.

John Wesley believed that these acts of devotion to Christ—or Means of Grace—were ways to grow in the grace of God. The key to Christian growth is not about how we feel but about our faithfulness. If left up to our feelings we would probably have days when we would not feel like praying or reading scripture. But faithfulness calls us to the Means of Grace whether we feel like it or not!

God is faithful in providing the Means of Grace and we must be faithful practicing them. It is in practicing the Means of Grace that we connect with God. This is how we maintain our relationship with God. In any relationship we must maintain communication, take time for dialogue, share with and learn about the other person. And we must spend time in the person's presence. The same is true for our relationship with God. We maintain our relationship with God by spending time in God's presence.

The Means of Grace

- Worship
- Holy Communion
- Fasting
- Prayer
- Searching the Scriptures
- Christian Conferencing
- Works of Mercy

John Wesley received a letter from an itinerant preacher in the Americas who confessed that he was having trouble maintaining a spiritually disciplined life. Wesley replied, "O begin! Fix some part of every day for private exercises. Whether you like it or not, read and pray daily. It is for your life; there is no other way: else you will be a trifler all your days." Wesley himself kept set times of devotion for over sixty years.

Holy Living

"Therefore prepare you minds for action; discipline yourselves; set all your hope on the grace that Jesus Christ will bring you when he is revealed. Like obedient children, do not be conformed to the desires that you formerly had in ignorance. Instead, as he who called you is holy, be holy yourselves in all your conduct; for it is written 'You shall be holy for I am holy'" (1 Pet. 1:13-15).

We are called as disciples to live holy lives. Dallas Willard describes the disciples of Jesus as those who learn to be like him, who live their lives as Jesus would. These disciples learn how to walk with Jesus in every aspect of their lives.

> **"In the meantime, let all those who are real members of the Church, see that they walk holy and unblamable in all things 'Ye are the light of the world'! Ye are 'a city set upon a hill' and 'cannot be hid' O 'let your light shine before men'!"**
>
> John Wesley

Accountability

Accountable Discipleship groups or Covenant Discipleship groups often act today as class meetings did in Wesley's time. They are made up of members of a congregation or various congregations who meet—usually once a week—to give an account of their progress as disciples on life's journey.

Spiritual leaders should be a part of an Accountable Discipleship or Covenant Discipleship group. All leaders need help and support as they serve in their various roles within their families, communities, and the world. For more information on Covenant Discipleship visit www.gbod.org/covenantdiscipleship.

Reflection Questions

In what ways are you practicing the Means of Grace?

____

____

____

Are you part of a covenant group (Accountable Discipleship or Covenant Discipleship)? If not, why might you consider joining one?

Litany of Commitment to the General Rules: There is a litany of commitment to the Wesleyan General Rules in the addendum of this resource that you may consider using at your Board of Laity or other leadership meetings.

Spiritual Gifts

"Like good stewards of the manifold grace of God, serve one another with whatever gift each of you has received. Whoever speaks must do so as one speaking the very words of God; whoever serves must do so with the strength that God supplies, so that God may be glorified in all things through Jesus Christ" (1 Pet. 4:10-11).

As a leader it is important to continue to develop your leadership skills. One way to do this is to discover or rediscover your spiritual gifts. Our spiritual gifts can change as we grow in our faith and in our discipleship. Encourage others to discover their gifts so that they can find the ways God has prepared them to serve in the areas of mission and ministry for which they have a passion.

Servant Leadership

As disciples we should be willing to serve as Jesus did, humbly and without resentment. Here is an example: A rider on horseback, many years ago, came upon a squad of soldiers who were trying to move a heavy piece of timber. A corporal lorded over the soldiers saying, "Heave," but the piece of timber was too heavy for the squad. "Why don't you help them?" asked the quiet man who had come upon the soldiers. "Me? Why, I am a corporal sir!" The stranger dismounted his horse and carefully took his place with the soldiers. "Now, all together boys, heave!" he said. And the large piece of timber slid into place. The stranger got back on his horse and addressed the corporal, "The next time you have a piece of timber for your men to handle, corporal, send for the commander-in-chief." It turned out that the man on the horse was George Washington.

Moses was a great leader. The Bible describes Moses as the most humble man on earth (Num. 12:3). This is why God called him to lead the Israelites out of slavery into the Promised Land. Jesus modeled servanthood to twelve men and changed the world. (Adapted from the writings of Danny Hernaez, used by permission.)

"Whoever wishes to be great among you must be your servant, and whoever wishes to be first among you must be your slave; just as the Son of Man came not to be served but to serve, and to give his life a ransom for many" (Matt. 20:26-28).

Servant leadership is a matter of prestige versus passion. Do you seek the prestige of a leadership position? Do you feel that it will make you important in the eyes of others? Or do you have a passion to provide leadership that will make a difference in your district or annual conference? Do you want to be intentional in your leadership to lead the way forward?

Reflection Questions

What qualities would you like to embody as a servant leader?

____

____

____

What steps might you take to ensure that you lead from a place of passion and not from a place of prestige?

____

Pray that God makes you a humble servant leader of others.

Adaptive Leadership

Adaptive leadership is the method of helping people face difficult and challenging situations and grow as a result of such circumstances. Leaders should understand the importance of adapting and they should be able to use these processes to help their groups not only survive a crisis but thrive as a result of it.

Adaptive leadership is characterized by keeping whatever is necessary for survival, discarding or changing what is no longer necessary, and creating new practices that will enable renewal and vitality.

To help your group or organization thrive, you must learn to adapt to your circumstances and stay focused on what is best about the situation (Appreciative Inquiry). In this process, the core values, purpose, and history of the entity must be appreciated and considered.

Adaptive leaders are people who do the following:

- Think and act to exert strategic influence in their various communities;
- Are proactive, foresee opportunities, and work to find resources to successfully develop those opportunities;
- Are flexible in their leadership style;
- Consider all aspects of a problem or situation and the various views, beliefs, or standards related to it when making decisions;
- Can accept the notion that they may be wrong in their approach and change or discard a course of action;
- Have a thorough knowledge of their entities/environments;
- Can create unique options for action;
- Build the capacities to learn, transform, change culture, and adapt technology as needed within their sphere of influence;
- Are willing to try new ways of doing things and do not fear failure;

- Are lifelong learners who are open to creative ideas and willing to improve their leadership abilities;
- Love and encourage creative ideas and processes from others.

Skills, Attitudes, and Qualities of Adaptive Leaders

An adaptive leader is a person who does the following:

- Keeps the core values and vision of a group connected with necessary changes in processes or procedures;
- Seeks to foster a culture that honors diversity of opinion for the good of the group;
- Understands that change and learning can be painful for people, and he or she anticipates reluctant behavior related to this pain;
- Understands that most change is a process that is/should be accomplished in stages. The leader should remain constant and resist the temptation to cut corners.

Unity in Ministry

"There is one body and one Spirit, just as you were called to the one hope of your calling, one Lord, one faith, one baptism, one God and Father of all, who is above all and through all and in all" (Eph. 4:4-6).

The ministry of **ALL** Christians is complementary. No ministry is subservient to another. All United Methodists are summoned and sent by Christ to live and work together in mutual interdependence, and they are to be guided by the Spirit into the truth that frees and the love that reconciles.

All roles are important in the church. Bishops, Conference Lay Leaders, district superintendents, District Lay Leaders, Local Church Lay Leaders, and pastors are all called to be in mission and ministry together.

God gives each of us diverse gifts and no one person has them all. Ephesians 4:11-13 tells us that some of us will be called to be apostles, prophets, evangelists, pastors, and teachers to prepare God's people for works of service, so that the body of Christ may be built up until we all reach unity in the faith. But none of us are called to be all these things. The letter goes on to say, "[F]rom whom the whole body, joined and knit together by every ligament with which it is equipped, as each part is working properly, promotes the body's growth in building itself up in love" (Eph. 4:16).

Be in prayer for your clergy leader. Ask to meet with him or her to discuss the needs of the church, district, or annual conference. Be as willing to listen as you are willing to speak. Do not be defensive or offensive. Be courteous and kind in order to develop a trusting and respectful relationship. Do not get caught up in conversations that demean or tear down your clergy leader. If someone has a problem with your clergy leader, ask the person to meet with him or her (you may even offer to accompany them if they would like).

Treat your clergy leader as you would like to be treated.

Mentoring New Leaders

A servant leader must recognize when God is raising new leadership, and they must affirm and encourage it. Servant leaders model a level of humility that God blesses. Leaders who are insecure in their positions might put down new leadership in order to maintain their own status.

In Numbers 11 we find that Joshua is concerned that two young men prophesied in the camp and considered this an affront to Moses' leadership: "But Moses said to him, 'Are you jealous for my sake? Would that all the Lord's people were prophets, and that the Lord would put his Spirit on them!'" (v. 29).

Moses viewed the situation differently. Moses looked at the situation with the eye of a servant leader and modeled humility and spiritual focus. Moses was secure in his leadership and did not need to put others down in order to feel secure.

The body of Christ needs leaders who are secure in their leadership. If God has called you to be a leader, look for opportunities to encourage new leaders. As you do, God will insure that you will fulfill the purpose for which God called you.

Mentor youth and young adults in whom you see potential. Be sure to include a variety of individuals as committee members. Diversity and inclusiveness are critical to the leadership of the church.

No one should remain in a position of leadership for an extended period of time. New leaders bring a fresh approach. It may take new leaders time to adapt to their new roles. This is why it is important to mentor potential leaders and involve them in the work of leadership in as many ways as possible. Ask for an associate leader to help with the multiple tasks of leadership roles in the conference, district, or local congregation. Find ways to partner to improve the overall leadership and fulfillment of responsibilities.

Reflection Questions

How flexible is your present leadership style? In what ways might you change your leadership style in order to lead more effectively?

____

____

____

In what ways can you improve your relationship with your clergy leader?

____

____

____

Who are persons that you could mentor and prepare for leadership roles?

____

____

____

Pray for the Holy Spirit to guide you in your leadership.

Effective Lay Leadership

Effective lay leadership is a marker of vital congregations that came out of a study conducted by The United Methodist Church called "A Call to Action."

What makes an effective Lay Leader? An effective Lay Leader is a spiritually grounded person who practices spiritual disciplines and participates in a covenant or accountability group. He or she engages in continuous study, reaches beyond the congregation in mission and ministry, and mentors others. Effective Lay Leaders use their spiritual gifts and encourage others to do so as well. They are willing to serve and they do not seek positions of leadership out of prestige.

The Virginia Annual Conference has developed a document on effective lay leadership called "Characteristics of Effective Lay Leadership in the Churches of the Virginia Conference." Below are some highlights from the document.

Leaders model what it means to be a disciple of Jesus Christ.

PRIMARY COMMITMENTS

- Leaders recognize that commitment to Jesus Christ is the foundation for all leadership in the church, and that commitment to God's will is the beginning of all vision.
- They recognize making disciples of Jesus Christ as the primary goal of the Church and of individual Christians.
- They see those who are closest to them—their family and friends—as the frontline arena for their ministry/service, and they commit to give them the best of themselves rather than the leftovers.

CHARACTER

- Leaders seek to respond to conflict as Jesus did—directly, openly, and responsibly, treating others with respect and always seeking justice, healthy accountability, and reconciliation.
- They recognize the importance of character and seek to become people whose lives are marked by integrity and compassion, and who treat others with respect regardless of their race, gender, social status, theological viewpoint, or any other human difference.
- They intentionally pursue spiritual growth and renewal of body, mind, and spirit, setting aside time to deepen their relationship with God and to grow in faith and discipleship.

LEADERSHIP STYLE

- Leaders are determined to be servant leaders, seeking the good of the kingdom rather than their own power and status, and they make decisions based on the good of the whole church rather than their own preferences.
- They listen to God, to the community, to their congregation, and to others of differing viewpoints, as well as to their own hearts, as they discern visions and set goals for their church's future and ministry.
- They are future-oriented, willing to take risks as they encourage others to celebrate the past while moving toward the future.
- They partner with their pastors—praying for, supporting, and encouraging them, and dealing honestly and openly with difficult issues.
- They seek to identify, nurture, encourage, and support leadership in others.

For more information visit the Virginia Annual Conference website: **www.vaumc.org.**

Reflection Questions

How would you rate yourself as an effective leader?

____

____

____

What steps might you take to become more effective?

____

____

____

Lay Servant Ministries

Lay Servant Ministries is a conference-based system for training and mobilizing laity for services of leading, caring, and communicating in the local congregation, the connectional church, and the community. It is highly recommended that Lay Leaders at all levels, lay members of the annual conference, and others seeking to prepare themselves for service be certified Lay Servants.

The conference director is responsible for oversight of Lay Servant Ministries. The Conference Committee on Lay Servant Ministries—including district directors—is responsible for seeing that training occurs regularly at the conference or district level, for approving locally developed teaching resources, for training and approving teachers of LSM, for setting conference rules, for carrying out the requirements of the *Book of Discipline* relating to Lay Servant Ministries, such as the role of Lay Speaker, and for approving other training that can substitute for re-certification of Lay Servants. Most of the actual organizational work and teaching of Lay Servant classes occurs at the district level.

Position Descriptions

Conference Lay Leader

The Conference Lay Leader chairs the Conference Board of Laity.

A Conference Lay Leader is a person who has experience in lay leadership positions within the local church and district. This person is aware of the responsibilities of the position and must be aware of the role of laity in mission and ministry within the congregation and the district and annual conference, as well as the opportunities for witness and mission through their ministries in the home, workplace, community, and world. The Conference Lay Leader provides direction both spiritually and procedurally to the Conference Board of Laity and Conference Committee on Lay Servant Ministries in cooperation with the Annual Conference Director of Lay Servant* Ministries. *(This title will be finalized when annual and central conferences ratify the constitutional change which lists the Conference Director of Lay Speaking Ministries as a member of the annual conference session.)

The Conference Lay Leader is a member of the annual conference sessions, and he or she should attend the annual conference sessions unless prevented. Membership on other conference related committees are the Conference Council on Ministries or equivalent structure; the Executive Committee (if existing) and/or the Extended Cabinet or equivalent structure; Conference Committee on Nominations; Conference Committee on Episcopacy; and the Committee on Planning Annual Conference Sessions

Some of these commitments may be shared with an associate Conference Lay Leader.

Expected results: An effective Conference Lay Leader works with the Annual Conference Board of Laity to enable and support lay participation in the planning and decision-making processes of the annual conference, districts, and local congregations in cooperation with the bishop, district superintendents, and pastors of local congregations.

As chair of the Conference Board of Laity, the Conference Lay Leader relates to the organized lay groups within the annual conference and supports their ministries.

The Conference Lay Leader works with the District Lay Leaders to develop the advocacy role for laity in the life of the church and encourage and equip laity in the general ministry of the church.

The Conference Lay Leader meets with the cabinet on matters of programming within the annual conference and meets regularly with the bishop to discuss the state of the annual conference and needs for ministry both locally and globally.

Qualifications

Spiritual gifts: Encouragement (exhortation), leadership, wisdom, discernment, apostleship, administration, shepherding, teaching.

Experience/skills: It is recommended that the Conference Lay Leader be a certified Lay Servant, and he or she should have experience in leadership at the district level and/or conference level. Some experience in leadership, ability to communicate effectively, good listening skills, organizational skills, ability to share vision, set goals, and monitor progress and lead meetings.

Responsibilities

- Commit to support the laity (Lay Servants and others) in spiritual formation and development of their roles in ministry and discipleship to help develop vital congregations and increase missional presence in the community
- Train District Lay Leaders in their roles
- Along with the Conference Board of Laity and the Conference Committee on Lay Servant Ministries interpret the needs of the annual conference for training opportunities
- In conjunction with the district superintendents recruit qualified District Lay Leaders who are gifted and equipped for leadership tasks
- Support District Lay Leaders as they equip Local Church Lay Leaders and other laity
- Nurture and support Lay Leaders and others in their various roles
- Communicate regularly with district and Local Church Lay Leaders

- Provide for forms of recognition for laity in leadership roles within the annual conference, including Lay Servants, Lay Speakers, and certified Lay Ministers
- Present a report to the annual conference
- Participate in the Service of Ordination at the annual conference session
- Become a member of the Association of Annual Conference Lay Leaders (AACLL)
- Chair the Conference Board of Laity

(See the Appreciative Inquiry Worksheets in the addendum of this resource to assess your work.)

Conference Board of Laity

The members of this board are the Conference Lay Leader, associate Conference Lay Leaders, Conference Director of Lay Servant Ministries,* conference scouting coordinator, and the presidents and two representatives elected by each of the conference organizations of United Methodist Men, United Methodist Women, United Methodist Young Adults, and the conference council on youth ministries, and in addition, the District Lay Leaders, two laymen, two lay women, and two youth elected by the annual conference upon nomination of the conference nominating committee, a district superintendent designated by the cabinet, the director of the conference council on ministries, and the presiding bishop.

The Conference Board of Laity is chaired by the Conference Lay Leader. Officers may be elected by the board as it deems necessary. Information on this board can be found in the *Book of Discipline*, the Annual Conference paragraphs (600+).

Responsibilities

The Conference Board of Laity relates to Lay Servant Ministries and other organized lay groups within the conference and supports their work by coordinating activities within the conference.

The overall purposes of this board are the following:

- Maintain connectional relationships within the annual conference and beyond
- Provide for the ministry of the laity related to the objectives of the General Board of Discipleship as set forth in paragraphs 1100+ of the *Book of Discipline*
- Foster an awareness of the role of laity within local congregations and ministries in the home, workplace, community, and the world

- Develop and promote programs
- Cultivate an adequate understanding of the theology and biblical basis for lay life and work among members of the churches within the annual conference
- Develop and promote stewardship of time, talent, and possessions within the annual conference in cooperation with the Conference Council on Ministries
- Provide for the training of lay members of the annual conference
- Provide support and direction for the ministry of the laity on the local, district, and annual conference levels and promote observance of Laity Sunday
- Provide organization, direction, and support for development of local church leaders
- Devote special attention to the inclusion of persons with disabilities and persons from a variety of racial and ethnic backgrounds
- Be a professing member of a local church

(See the Appreciative Inquiry Worksheets in the addendum of this resource to assess your work.)

District Lay Leader

The District Lay Leader is a key position for equipping the laity of the district/annual conference.

Expected Results: An effective District Lay Leader works with the District Board of Laity to foster the awareness of the role of laity both within congregations and through their ministries in the home, workplace, community, and world. He or she supports and enables the participation of the laity in the planning and decision-making processes of the district and local churches in cooperation with the district superintendent and pastors. The District Lay Leader provides training for Local Church Lay Leaders and their ministries in local churches. He or she also participates in congregational or cluster charge conferences along with the district superintendent.

Qualifications

Spiritual gifts: Encouragement (exhortation), leadership, wisdom, discernment, apostleship, administration, shepherding, teaching.

Experience/skills: Must be a professing member of a local congregation, and it is recommended that he or she be a certified Lay Servant; should have experience in leadership at the district level and local congregation in which he or she holds membership. Some experience in leadership, ability to communicate effectively, good listening skills, organizational skills, ability to share vision, set goals, and monitor progress

Responsibilities

- Commit to support the laity of the district in spiritual formation and promote the ministry of the laity within congregations and the district to help develop vital congregations and increase our missional presence in the community
- Equip Local Church Lay Leaders for their leadership roles
- Along with the District Director of Lay Servant Ministries interpret the needs of the district laity for training opportunities
- Relate to organized lay groups—United Methodist Men, United Methodist Women, and the like—and support their work
- Attend annual conference sessions unless prevented
- District Council on Ministries
- District Conference and Executive Committee
- Committee on District Superintendency
- District Committee on Lay Servant Ministries
- Conference Board of Laity
- May have an associate District Lay Leader share some of the responsibilities listed here
- Chair the District Board of Laity

(See the Appreciative Inquiry Worksheets in the addendum of this resource to assess your work.)

District Board of Laity

The District Board of Laity relates to the annual conference through the Conference Board of Laity. The District Board of Laity is chaired by the District Lay leader. Membership includes the District Lay Leader, associate District Lay Leader(s), the District Director of Lay Servant Ministries, and may include the district superintendent, district president of United Methodist Women, district president of United Methodist Men, district president of United Methodist Youth, district president of United Methodist Young Adults, and the district president of the Older Adult Council (where organized), and others as necessary. The role of this committee can be found in the *Book of Discipline* under The District Conference paragraphs (600+).

Responsibilities

To work with the District Lay Leader in the following areas:

- Developing and promoting an increased role for laity in the life of the local church
- Increasing the participation of laity in the sessions and programs of the district and local churches in cooperation with the district superintendent and pastors
- Encouraging laypersons to participate in the general ministry of the church in the world
- Equip Local Church Lay Leaders for their leadership roles
- Equip others in leadership positions within local congregations
- Encourage working relationships between laity and pastors
- Develop and promote stewardship of time, talent, and possessions within the district in cooperation with the District Council on Ministries
- Relate to the Lay Servant Ministries program

Spiritual gifts: Encouragement (exhortation), leadership, wisdom, discernment, apostleship, administration, shepherding, teaching

Experience/skills: It is recommended that the District Lay Leader be a certified Lay Servant and have experience in leadership at the district level. It would be beneficial for this person to have been a member of the District Board of Laity.

Some experience in leadership, ability to communicate effectively, good listening skills, organizational skills, ability to share vision, set goals, and monitor progress and lead meetings

(See the Appreciative Inquiry Worksheets in the addendum of this resource to assess your work.)

Local Church Lay Leaders

It is the responsibility of the District Lay Leader to train and equip the Local Church Lay Leaders within their district. You can find additional information on the role of the Local Church Lay Leader in the *Guidelines for Leading Your Congregation 2013-2016: Lay Leader/Lay Member* available from Cokesbury and *Job Descriptions and Leadership Training in The United Methodist Church—2013-2016* available from Discipleship Resources. There is a PowerPoint presentation available for training Local Church Lay Leaders and lay members based on the *Lay Leader/Lay Member* resource. It can be found at www.gbod.org/laity.

Responsibilities

- Advocacy—represent the laity of the congregation and act as an extension of the congregation in the community
- Model discipleship—demonstrate faith and integrity, and continue to study and meet with a covenant group
- Build awareness—foster the ministry of the laity, recognize and celebrate the ministry of the laity, promote service opportunities and educational opportunities
- Exemplify leadership—serve as coleader with appointed leader (pastor); includes meeting regularly with the pastor
- Service—serve on various committees, assist the church council
- Commitment—member of charge conference, church council, finance committee, nominations and leadership development committee (may serve as cochair)
- Staff/Pastor Parish Relations Committee

(See the Appreciative Inquiry Worksheets in the addendum of this resource to assess your work.)

Leading Meetings

As chair of the Board of Laity within the annual conference or district you will be the person responsible for leading the meetings of these groups as well as others. The way a meeting is led can make the difference between a dull, unproductive meeting and one that is energizing and has a realistic purpose and achievable goals.

Christian or Holy Conferencing

"And let us consider how to provoke one another to love and good deeds, not neglecting to meet together, as is the habit of some, but encouraging one another, and all the more as you see the Day approaching" (Heb. 10:24-25).

John Wesley considered Christian conferencing a Means of Grace, or one of the ways in which we can grow in relationship to God. Conferencing is an important part of our United Methodist heritage. Each congregation has its own charge conference and annual conference, jurisdictional conference, and general conference. The way these meetings are conducted is what makes us as Christians different from the rest of the world. But are we different?

Christian conferencing involves meeting regularly with other Christians for the purpose of conversation, teaching, accountability, mutual encouragement, and support for discipleship. In Christian conferencing, disciples provide mutual support for one another and help one another be accountable so they can grow in their love of God and neighbor.

Imagine how the tone of meetings could change if they became a time of Christian conferencing. Imagine looking forward to a meeting because you know it will be a time of mutual encouragement, prayer, and Bible study. Imagine the work you could accomplish if you took time to attune yourself to the Holy Spirit and seek the Spirit's guidance in your work.

In *Discerning God's Will Together*, Danny Morris and Charles Olsen say, "Litanies of committee reports held together by bookend prayers create predictable and sterile meetings." Consider the positive consequences of using each time you hold a meeting to practice the Means of Grace in order to grow in your discipleship. It could transform your meetings entirely.

You might also consider tithing your meeting time for every hour you meet (six minutes should be spent in prayer, and so on).

Here is a suggested meeting process:

- Light a Christ candle
- Brief devotion/scripture reading
- Hymn or chorus
- Responsive reading
- Prayer concerns
- Pray over the agenda and concerns spoken by those attending the meeting
- Seeks God's guidance as you work through the items on your agenda

Meetings involve worshipful work. When you plan opportunities for worship—prayers, hymns, affirmations of faith, Bible study, storytelling, silence, and celebration—the meeting becomes a worshipful experience through the presence of the Holy Spirit. When leaders consciously offer their agenda to God the meeting place becomes holy ground, just as the sanctuary does during worship.

Discernment

Discernment occurs when we focus on God's purpose for the meeting.

Samuel listened to God's voice to discern which of Jesse's sons would be anointed king, and Solomon asked God for a wise and discerning mind. Romans 12:2 says, "Do not be conformed to this world, but be transformed by the renewing of your minds so that you may discern what is the will of God—what is good and acceptable and perfect." One of the spiritual gifts listed in 1 Cor. 12:10 is the discernment between spirits. 1 John 4:1 says, "Beloved, do not believe every spirit, but test [discern] the spirits to see whether they are from God." Early Christians feared false prophets and tested the spirits to determine if they were from God.

The purpose and goal of spiritual discernment is to *know* God's will so that we can *do* God's will. We must keep our eyes and our hearts on this purpose and goal. We must not ignore the idea of discernment in our decision-making processes today.

Holy conferencing should be the manner in which we govern our life together. It emphasizes fellowship within the body of Christ. Holy conferencing calls us to build one another up and not tear one another down.

Parliamentary procedure is a process often used to govern meetings and make decisions. When we use Parliamentary procedure we employ motions and amend amendments, and we vote on this or that. The problem with this kind of process is that it can divide us and create a win/lose situation. Parliamentary procedure creates a competitive dynamic where ideas are owned and defended. And if the presider is not an expert in Parliamentary procedure the meeting can get out of hand.

Consensus, an idea seen often throughout scripture, creates a more cooperative dynamic than Parliamentary procedure. The purpose of consensus is to discover the best possible decision for the group. Consensus requires practice and expertise but seeks solutions that best meet the needs of the whole group. Consensus may require group members to "stand aside" though they disagree. In consensus, the ideal outcome for the group is considered above an individual opinion. Consensus desires God's plan over our own desires.

Discerning a Way Forward

During your leadership it is important to lead your teams or committees in a time of discerning a plan for your work. One process you can use is the CAP Experience: Current Reality, Assets and Abilities, and Potential Partners.

- Current Reality: look at things the way they are right now then assess needed changes
- Assets and Abilities: spiritual gifts, personal or material resources, opportunities, programs, and the like
- Potential Partners: other organizations in the conference, community, and the like, who could partner to provide resources, and so forth

Organizing Your Board of Laity

Here are some points to consider as you organize your group.

Check the *Book of Discipline* and your annual conference organizational chart to determine who is required to be at the table.

- Schedule a date and location for organizing the Board of Laity with the district superintendent or cabinet member assigned to your board.
- Add the date to the district calendar and/or the conference calendar.
- Invite the Conference Director or District Director of Lay Servant Ministries to attend.
- Publicize the meeting on the conference website or district website and in the conference newsletter or district newsletter.

Here is a suggested agenda for the organizational meeting.

- Opening devotions/singing—set the stage for Christian conferencing
- Explain the purpose of the meeting
- Explain the membership of the Board of Laity (See the requirements in the *Book of Discipline*)
- Provide training on the purpose and function of the Board of Laity
- Compare the purpose of the Board of Laity with the work of other committees or groups
- Lead a time of discernment on what your goals will be (use the CAP experience)
- Plan the next meeting
- Discuss the frequency of meetings
- Define the purpose of the next meeting
- Discuss how training will happen for district and Local Church Lay Leaders (there is a PowerPoint presentation available from GBOD for each of these training needs, www.gbod.org/laity)
- Identify other training needs and discuss whether there are other laity-empowering events that would be helpful
- End with prayer and song, "Commitment to the General Rules" (see addendum), and/or "A Covenant Prayer in the Wesleyan Tradition" (*UMH*, no. 607)

Leading Change

As leader, one of your responsibilities includes leading change (not maintaining the status quo!). During your meetings it will be important that you do the following:

- Develop or review your mission and vision
- Review strategic initiatives of the annual conference
- Define measurable goals
- Develop plans of action
- Evaluate your progress

Appreciative Inquiry: A New Way of Thinking

"Finally, beloved, whatever is true, whatever is honorable, whatever is just, whatever is pure, whatever is pleasing, whatever is commendable, if there is any excellence and if there is anything worthy of praise, think about these things" (Phil. 4:8).

Appreciative Inquiry and Asset Based Community Development are important processes in leading change. Appreciative Inquiry is a way of seeing things as they are and creating a plan for the future. It is a way of forming a community that can perceive, think, and create with their best life resources. Appreciative Inquiry offers a different reality from the current one, as well as a different way of perceiving and living.

We tend to take the traditional approach to problem solving by focusing on what we do not have—our lack of resources, our failure to achieve, and our "neediness." But with the Appreciative Inquiry, we learn to appreciate and value the best of what we have. We envision what might be and we engage in dialogue about what should be. This ultimately leads to innovation.

Appreciative Inquiry assumes that in every group or organization there is something that works. It acknowledges that our focus becomes our reality. If we focus on our problems, failures, and deficits, this will become our reality. If we focus on our successes, assets, and gifts, this will become our reality instead.

Appreciative Inquiry assumes that people have more confidence in journeying into the future if they can bring with them parts of the past. If we carry our past with us, it must only be that which is good. Otherwise our negative thoughts and processes from the past will weigh us down in the future. We must focus on the positive!

Asset Based Community Development: How We Work with Other Partners

Asset Based Community Development (ABCD) is a process of identifying possible partners for action. Those partners are identified by interviewing persons within the congregation and community in an attempt to discover the gifts and assets that each person possesses. ABCD asks the following questions:

- What are your best gifts?
- What do you love doing and what do you do well?
- What are the big changes of which you would like to be a part?
- How do you see your role in these changes?

ABCD connects people with others who have common motivations. Asset Mapping involves identifying the actual gifts or assets that are available around you. These assets can include individuals, associations, and institutions.

You should seek to discover the answers to the following questions in each of these:

- What do they currently do?
- What have they talked about doing but have not yet done?
- What might they do if they were asked?
- What are their gifts?
- What physical space and equipment exists?
- How is money spent (supplies, services, hiring, and the like)?
- What is their current relationship with the community?

This process will help you discover resources that could be used for your mission or ministry. Lack of resources must not become the focus of our discussions on planning and creating. Assets abound to help us achieve our goals, we just have to find them!

Reflection Questions

Recall a time when an Appreciative Inquiry approach could have created positive energy in a meeting.

____

____

____

How will you use AI and ABCD in your planning processes?

____

____

____

The Way Forward

In order to bring about change or move forward we must have a plan. We need a vision of where we are going—a defined mission of what we plan to accomplish and goals to guide us along the way.

- Vision—who we are to be (how we want to be known)
- Mission—our purpose (what we are to do)
- Values—our guiding principles and beliefs underlying our opinions, attitudes, and behaviors (why we think and act as we do)

Shared Vision

Visions are best when shared (and agreed upon!). A shared vision reflects the mission and values of the group. We are motivated by beliefs and goals we hold most sacred and in common with one another.

A shared vision does the following:

- Offers a picture of what the organization will look like in the future
- Appeals to the long-term interest of all those who are engaged in it
- Guides decision making
- Permits individual initiative
- Allows itself to be communicated easily

George Barna says that leadership is the process of motivating, mobilizing, resourcing, and directing people. Leadership helps people passionately and strategically pursue a vision from God that the group embraces. It is more than administration, doing things right, doing the right things, or management. Leadership is the process of working with others in the development of a shared vision and then enabling the articulation of that vision. It is one thing to develop a vision but another thing to bring that vision to fruition.

Consider the following scene from Alice in Wonderland:

Alice: "Would you tell me, please, which way I ought to go from here?"
Cheshire Cat: "That depends a good deal on where you want to get to."
Alice: "I don't much care where—"
Cheshire Cat: "Then it doesn't matter which way you go."
(*Alice in Wonderland*, Lewis Carroll)

We must first know where we are going! Then we can decide which road will get us there.

There will always be issues before us. But these issues are less dominating when we share a vision, focus on it, and set goals that will allow us to accomplish that vision. It is important that our vision be shared by others. When we share the same goals and work for the same outcome, our vision becomes a powerful force. We have to believe that we can do it! The letter to the Ephesians says, "Now to him who by the power at work within us is able to accomplish abundantly far more than all we can ask or imagine, to him be glory in the church and in Christ Jesus to all generations, forever and ever. Amen" (3:20-21).

Current Reality and Desired Reality

In order to develop a vision, mission, or goals, you have to understand where you are right now. And you need to know where you want to go and what you hope for in the future.

In order to understand your current reality you must answer the questions below:

- What are you hearing in the church?
- What are you hearing about the church?

Current reality is the thoughts, ideas, memories, perspectives, rituals, practices, processes, procedures, and resources of an individual or group. Current reality is fluid and always changing. The current reality today might not be the current reality tomorrow.

Our desired reality is the way we would like things to be. The desired reality of a group is like a motion picture, not a photograph. It is rich, textured, multilayered, and panoramic.

As we think about our desired reality, we should do so in light of God's plan—what God would have us to do. This is why discerning God's will is critical in developing our way forward. God's vision is beyond our own limited vision.

Here is a list of the characteristics of God's vision:

- Based on using us beyond our capacity
- Challenges us to accomplish an impossible or improbable dream
- Brings God delight
- Demonstrates God's power at work in us
- Drives us to our knees in humility and obedience
- Becomes an obsession we embrace
- Reflects biblical themes of people, holiness, love, and transformation

Goals

As you set goals for improvement, keep in mind the criteria to be met in order to meet your goals. In other words, be SMART by making your goals measurable!

Effective goals are:

Specific: clear and unambiguous and answer the five W's—*What, Why, Who, Where,* and *Which*

Measurable: answers the questions *How many? How Much? How will I know when it is accomplished?*

Achievable: Are they realistic? Can they be accomplished?

Relevant: Are they worthwhile? Do they match our needs and efforts?
Timed: What is the time frame for our goals to be met? What is the target date?

Action Steps

Action steps are the specific steps we will take to accomplish our goals. Setting goals is only helpful if we discuss and plan the steps needed to achieve these goals. Based on the goals we have set, our actions steps are designed to get us where we want to be.

Evaluating Progress

It is a good idea to check your progress frequently. When your goals are measurable and your action steps clear, you can review what has been done and assess your progress toward the completion of your goals. If your plans are not progressing as you hoped, it may be time to revise your goals and action steps. Flexibility is key to success.

Do not try this alone!

Find a prayer partner(s) who will pray for you regularly. Choose people you can trust and give them specific prayer concerns when possible. Leaders who are upheld with prayer have a better chance of providing faithful servant leadership.

Suggested Resources

The Book of Discipline of The United Methodist Church (current edition), The United Methodist Publishing House

Spiritual Leadership

Becoming Barnabas: The Ministry of Encouragement by Paul Moots, Alban Institute
John Wesley: Holiness of Heart and Life by Charles Yrigoyen Jr, Abingdon
The Soul of Tomorrow's Church by Kent Ira Groff, Upper Room Books
Spiritual Preparation for Christian Leadership by E. Glenn Hinson, Upper Room Books

Leading Meetings

Discerning God's Will Together: A Spiritual Practice for the Church by Danny E. Morris and Charles M. Olsen, Upper Room Books
Hearing with the Heart: A Gentle Guide to Discerning God's Will for Your Life by Debra K. Farrington, Josey-Bass

Appreciative Inquiry

Appreciative Inquiry Handbook by David L. Cooperrider et al., Berrett-Koehler Publishers
Memories, Hopes, and Conversations: Appreciative Inquiry and Congregational Change by Mark Lau Branson, Alban Institute

The Thin Book of Appreciative Inquiry by Sue Annis Hammond, Thin Book Publishing Company

Asset Based Community Development

Building Communities from the Inside Out by John P. Kretzman and John L. McKnight, ACTA Publishing

The Power of Asset Mapping by Luther Snow, Alban Institute

"ABCD in Action: When People Care Enough to Act" (pdf) www.mike-green.org/pub/abcd_book_introduction.pdf, http://www.mike-green.org, Mike Green, ABCD Trainer

Mission and Ministry

Introducing the Missional Church: What It Is, Why It Matters, How To Become One by Alan J. Roxburgh and M. Scott Boren, Baker Books

Missional Renaissance: Changing the Scorecard for the Church by Reggie McNeal, Josey-Bass

The Forgotten Ways by Alan Hirsch, Brazos Press

Missional: Joining God in the Neighborhood by Alan J. Roxburgh, Baker Books

Touch by Rudy Rasmus, Thomas Nelson

Not Just a One-Night Stand: Ministry with the Homeless by John Flowers and Karen Vannoy, Discipleship Resources

Leadership

The Starfish and the Spider: The Unstoppable Power of Leaderless Organizations by Ori Brafman and Rod A. Beckstrom, Portfolio Trade

The Practice of Adaptive Leadership: Tools and Tactics for Changing Your Organization and the World by Ronald A. Heifetz and Marty Linsky, Harvard Business Review

Switch: How to Change Things When Change Is Hard by Chip Heath and Dan Heath, Broadway Books

ADDENDUM

Litany of Commitment to the General Rules*

Leader: The grace of God resounds with the truth that a life of faith calls us to live our baptism daily as faithful disciples of Jesus Christ. From the earliest days we Methodists have declared that our essential life and witness are rooted in three simple yet world-changing General Rules.

People: By the grace of God, we will seek to embody God's love in all that we do and say, and by the same grace seek to fulfill three general rules in our daily living.

Leader: Will we then, sisters and brothers, commit ourselves first to do no harm?

People: We commit ourselves to resist evil and injustice wherever we find it in ourselves and in the world around us. May the way we live never cause another to stumble or to turn away from You, O Lord.

Leader: Will we next commit ourselves to do all the good we can?

People: We commit ourselves to pay attention to others doing good for their souls and bodies, and by persevering in love bring healing and hope into all relationships.

Leader: Finally, will we faithfully use the means of God, what John Wesley called the "ordinances of God"?

People: We commit ourselves to regular worship and daily prayer, to the searching of your Word, to deeper participation in the Lord's Supper, and to keep our appointments with You as we grow closer to you, our loving and redeeming Lord. Amen.

*Based on a litany by Reverend Robert Milsom, Cornwall United Methodist Church, New York

Appreciative Inquiry Worksheets

Conference Lay Leader

How can you be spiritually prepared for your role?	What is working well? __________ __________ __________ How can it work better? __________ __________ __________ What resources are available to help achieve success?
Fostering awareness of the role of laity both within the congregation and through their ministries in the home, workplace, community, and world	What is working well? __________ __________ __________ How can it work better? __________ __________ __________ What resources are available to help achieve success?

The Conference Lay Leader shall also have the general responsibility in: • Developing the advocacy role for the laity in the life of the church	What is working well? ____________________ ____________________ ____________________ How can it work better? ____________________ ____________________ ____________________ What resources are available to help achieve success?
Increasing the participation of the laity in the sessions and structure of annual conference Encouraging laypersons in the general ministry of the church	What is working well? ____________________ ____________________ ____________________ How can it work better? ____________________ ____________________ ____________________ What resources are available to help achieve success?
The Conference Lay Leader shall chair the Conference Board of Laity or equivalent structure	What is working well? ____________________ ____________________ ____________________ How can it work better? ____________________ ____________________ ____________________ What resources are available to help achieve success?

The Conference Lay Leader shall be responsible for presenting a report to the annual conference	What is working well? __________ __________ __________ How can it work better? __________ __________ __________ What resources are available to help achieve success?
The Conference Lay Leader **may** serve on the Board of Ordained Ministry and will participate in the Service of Ordination at annual conference	What is working well? __________ __________ __________ How can it work better? __________ __________ __________ What resources are available to help achieve success?
The Conference Lay Leader shall meet with the cabinet when matters relating to the coordination, implementation, or administration of the conference program or other matters as the cabinet may determine are on the agenda	What is working well? __________ __________ __________ How can it work better? __________ __________ __________ What resources are available to help achieve success?

The Annual Conference Lay Leader will meet regularly with the bishop to discuss the state of the annual conference, the church, and the needs for ministry both locally and globally	What is working well? __________ __________ __________ How can it work better? __________ __________ __________ What resources are available to help achieve success?
Spiritual Leadership versus Political Leadership How are you maintaining a spiritual focus in your work?	What is working well? __________ __________ __________ How can it work better? __________ __________ __________ What resources are available to help achieve success?
Meetings, meetings, meetings! How do we maintain balance between our other tasks per the *Discipline* and positional roles at meetings?	What is working well? __________ __________ __________ How can it work better? __________ __________ __________ What resources are available to help achieve success?

The conference Lay Leader and associate Lay Leader(s) will receive reasonable reimbursement for approved dues and expenses necessary for the ministry	What is working well? __________ __________ __________ How can it work better? __________ __________ __________ What resources are available to help achieve success?
The role of listener: Difficult—leaders need to let go of the status and control of being the "expert" The privilege of speaking not shared by all	What is working well? __________ __________ __________ How can it work better? __________ __________ __________ What resources are available to help achieve success?

Conference Board of Laity

• Relate to the organized lay groups in the conference such as UM, UMW, UMY and Scouting Min., encourage and support their work and activities	What is working well? __________ __________ __________ How can it work better? __________ __________ __________ What resources are available to help achieve success?
How does the Board of Laity work together to initiate projects/ministries that directly support the priorities of the annual conference? The Four Focus areas of the UMC?	What is working well? __________ __________ __________ How can it work better? __________ __________ __________ What resources are available to help achieve success?

Maintain connectional relationships within the annual conference and beyond	What is working well? How can it work better? What resources are available to help achieve success?
Foster an awareness of the role of laity within local congregation and ministries in the home, workplace, community, and the world	What is working well? How can it work better? What resources are available to help achieve success?
To develop and promote programs	What is working well? How can it work better? What resources are available to help achieve success?

Develop and promote stewardship of time, talent, and possessions within the AC in cooperation with the Conference Council on Ministries	What is working well? __________ __________ __________ How can it work better? __________ __________ __________ What resources are available to help achieve success?
Provide for the training of lay members of AC	What is working well? __________ __________ __________ How can it work better? __________ __________ __________ What resources are available to help achieve success?
Provide organization, direction, and support for development of local church leaders	What is working well? __________ __________ __________ How can it work better? __________ __________ __________ What resources are available to help achieve success?

Special attention should be given to the inclusion of people with disabilities and racial and ethnic persons	What is working well? __________ __________ __________ How can it work better? __________ __________ __________ What resources are available to help achieve success?

District Lay Leader

Fostering awareness of the role of laity both within their congregations and through their ministries in the home, workplace, community and the world in achieving the mission of the church	What is working well? __________ __________ __________ How can it work better? __________ __________ __________ What resources are available to help achieve success?
Supporting and enabling lay participation in the planning and decision making processes of the district and the local churches in cooperation with the district superintendent and pastors	What is working well? __________ __________ __________ How can it work better? __________ __________ __________ What resources are available to help achieve success?

Relate to organized lay groups, e.g. UMM, UMW, etc., and support their work	What is working well? __________ __________ __________ How can it work better? __________ __________ __________ What resources are available to help achieve success?
May designate persons to serve as proxy in the some groups **(see the *Book of Discipline*)**	What is working well? __________ __________ __________ How can it work better? __________ __________ __________ What resources are available to help achieve success?

District Board of Laity

Foster awareness of the role of laity within the local congregation and through their ministries in the home, workplace, community, and world in achieving the mission of the church	What is working well? ____________________ ____________________ ____________________ How can it work better? ____________________ ____________________ ____________________ What resources are available to help achieve success?
To work with the District Lay Leader in: • developing and promoting an increased role for laity in the life of the local church	What is working well? ____________________ ____________________ ____________________ How can it work better? ____________________ ____________________ ____________________ What resources are available to help achieve success?

• increasing the participation of laity in the sessions and programs of the district and local churches in cooperation with the district superintendent and pastors	What is working well? __________ __________ __________ How can it work better? __________ __________ __________ What resources are available to help achieve success?
• encouraging laypersons to participate in the general ministry of the church in the world	What is working well? __________ __________ __________ How can it work better? __________ __________ __________ What resources are available to help achieve success?
To develop and promote stewardship of time, talent, and possessions within the district in cooperation with the District Council on Ministries	What is working well? __________ __________ __________ How can it work better? __________ __________ __________ What resources are available to help achieve success?

Train Local Church Lay Leaders on how they can fulfill their roles	What is working well? __________ __________ __________ How can it work better? __________ __________ __________ What resources are available to help achieve success?
Equip Local Church Lay Leaders to energize and train the local church laity in what it means to be in ministry as a layperson	What is working well? __________ __________ __________ How can it work better? __________ __________ __________ What resources are available to help achieve success?
Provide a forum which will assist the District Ministry Team (the DS, the District Director of LSM, and the District Secretary) to identify training needs for the laity in the churches of the district	What is working well? __________ __________ __________ How can it work better? __________ __________ __________ What resources are available to help achieve success?

Local Church Lay Leader

Advocacy; represent the laity of the congregation, act as an extension of the congregation in the community	What is working well? __________ __________ __________ How can it work better? __________ __________ __________ What resources are available to help achieve success?
Model discipleship: model faith and integrity continue to study covenant group	What is working well? __________ __________ __________ How can it work better? __________ __________ __________ What resources are available to help achieve success?

Building Awareness: foster the ministry of the laity, recognize and celebrate the ministry of the laity, promote service and educational opportunities	What is working well? __________ __________ __________ How can it work better? __________ __________ __________ What resources are available to help achieve success?
Leadership example: can serve as co-leader with appointed leader (pastor), meets with the pastor	What is working well? __________ __________ __________ How can it work better? __________ __________ __________ What resources are available to help achieve success?
Assist the church council	What is working well? __________ __________ __________ How can it work better? __________ __________ __________ What resources are available to help achieve success?

Charge Conference—write report	What is working well? __________ __________ __________ How can it work better? __________ __________ __________ What resources are available to help achieve success?
Serve as Committee Member: Finance Committee, Nominations and Leadership Development Committee (may serve as co-chair) Staff/Pastor Parish Relations Committee	What is working well? __________ __________ __________ How can it work better? __________ __________ __________ What resources are available to help achieve success?

Printed in the USA
CPSIA information can be obtained
at www.ICGtesting.com
JSHW061159290924
70633JS00013B/144